b small publishing

SLIMY SCIENCE
AND
AWESOME EXPERIMENTS

Susan Martineau
Illustrations by Martin Ursell

Published by b small publishing,
Pinewood, 3a Coombe Ridings, Kingston upon Thames, Surrey KT2 7JT, UK
www.bsmall.co.uk
© b small publishing, 1999
US edition 2003
5 4 3 2 1

All rights reserved. No reproduction, copy or transmission of this publication may be made without written permission.
No part of this publication may be reproduced, stored in a retrieval system, or transmitted in any form or by any means, electronic, mechanical, photocopying,
recording or otherwise, without the prior permission of the publisher.

Printed in Hong Kong by Wing King Tong Co. Ltd.
ISBN 1 902915 90 9

Before You Begin

Most of the experiments give you pretty immediate and stunning results. Some of them take longer and need more patience —but they are worth it!

You don't need any special equipment to do the experiments, just things you probably have around the house—like old bottles, vinegar, aluminum foil, scissors, paper, and so on.

Read through the whole experiment before you begin. If it doesn't work the first time, try again! You could keep notes or even write up your results like a real professional.

Remember never to play with heat or chemicals, and don't forget to clean up afterward!

Always ask for permission before you start. Sometimes you will need help from a grown-up.

Sense-sational Science

Our senses of smell, sight, touch, and taste all play a vital part in telling us what things are. Is it edible? Is it fresh or stale? Is it bitter or sweet? See what happens when you can't use all of your senses to identify things.

Squidge 'n Sniff

Get your friends squishing their fingers in goop! You can choose your own gunky ideas, too, but remember to make sure no one tastes the stuff. Just squish and sniff!

What you will need:

- 5 small bowls or saucers
- 5 different squishy substances,
  e.g., honey, mustard, shampoo, ketchup, toothpaste
- scarf
- tissues

In each bowl or saucer add a different substance. Make sure your friends are not looking.

Lightly blindfold a brave friend with the scarf. Hold his finger and stick it into one of the substances.

Ask your friend to sniff the stuff on his finger and tell you what he thinks it is. Wipe the finger on a napkin and try another glob.

Weird or What?

One of the smelliest flowers ever is also the largest in the world. The rafflesia flower measures up to about 3 feet across and is found in Malaysia and Indonesia. It might look lovely, but it smells like rotting meat!

Tricky Tastebuds

This is a tricky test for your tastebuds. Try it on your family and friends. You could think of other foods to sample too.

What you will need:

- potato
- apple
- cucumber
- peeler and knife
- plate
- paper towel
- scarf

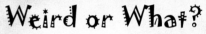

Weird or What?

When a toad is slurping up bugs, it can flick its tongue out and back again in one-tenth of a second.

1

Peel the fruit and veggies. Cut a few chunks of each. Make them about the same size.

paper towel

2

Put the chunks on a plate and cover them up. Do not let anyone see which is which.

3

Lightly blindfold a friend and ask him to hold his nose. Feed him a piece of each food and see if he can tell you what it is.

Fact File ▷▶

Your tastebuds are amazing! Touch the tip of your tongue with a clean, Popsicle stick and the wood will taste sweet. On the sides of your tongue it will taste sour.

Bouncing Light

Mirrors are great for magic effects. By holding them in different positions next to pictures or photos you can make things look very strange.

What you will need:

- glue
- school picture of yourself (or from a photo booth)
- small rectangular makeup mirror

1 Glue your photo on top of the face in the box below. Make sure the top of your head lines up with the horizontal line, and your nose is over the vertical one.

2 Stand one edge of the mirror on the vertical dotted line. Gradually slide it to the right—and you've conjured up a twin!

3 Now place the mirror on the horizontal line and—wow!—you're doing acrobatics.

Glue your photo on top of this face, in the same position.

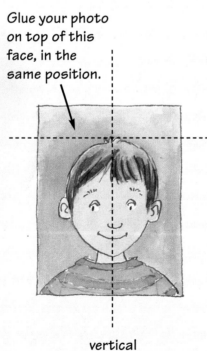

horizontal

vertical

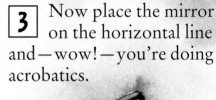

Weird or What?

Today's mirrors are made of a sheet of glass with a very thin coat of silver on the back. Before they were invented, people used polished metal to check how bad their zits were! For some weird reflections, look at yourself in each side of a shiny spoon.

Fact File ▷▶

In this experiment you see the photo in two different ways. When you look at the picture itself, light bounces directly off the photo into your eyes. But the image you see in the mirror is light bouncing off the photo, onto the shiny surface of the glass, and *then* into your eyes.

If you have two small mirrors, stand them on their edges facing each other, on each side of the photo. Count how many of you you can see.

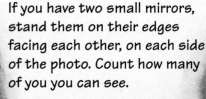

Mighty Magnifier

Make a simple magnifying glass with cardboard and plastic wrap. You could use this to inspect the results of your experiments like the Crystal Crust on page 11.

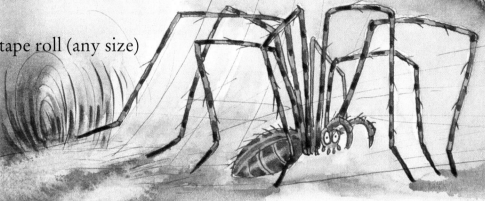

What you will need:

- cardboard or an empty tape roll (any size)
- scissors
- plastic wrap
- Scotch tape
- a dead insect (optional)

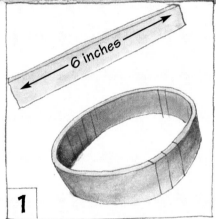

1

2

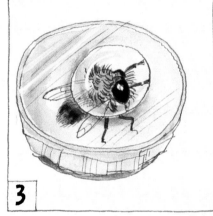

3

If using cardboard, cut a strip about 6 inches long. Tape the ends together to make a circle.

Cut a piece of plastic wrap big enough to cover and overlap the edges of the circle or empty tape roll. Keep it taut and tape down the sides.

Place the magnifier over the insect or the drawings below, and gently plop a few drops of water onto the plastic wrap. Look through the water at the superbugs!

Fact File ▷▶ The glass lens of a magnifying glass is curved and changes the angle of the rays of light. This makes things look larger and more detailed. Here the water works like a lens.

Eggsperiments

Floating Eyeball

Not for the faint-hearted!

What you will need:

- 1 uncooked fresh egg
- waterproof markers
- large glass jelly jar
- tablespoon
- lots of salt

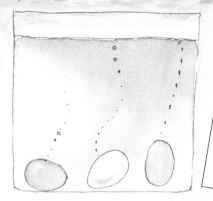

The Fresh Egg Test

Place an uncooked egg in a glass bowl of water. If it lies down horizontally then it is fresh. If one end starts to rise to the surface this means the egg has more air inside it and is less than fresh. An egg that stands up is not what you want for breakfast!

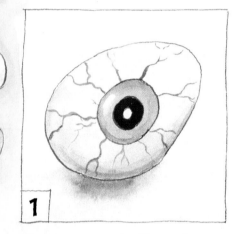

1

Draw an eyeball on the egg using the markers. Let the ink dry.

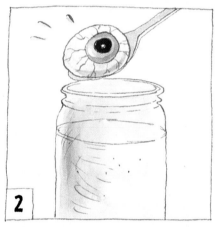

2

Fill the jelly jar with very warm water. Gently lower the egg into the jar using the spoon.

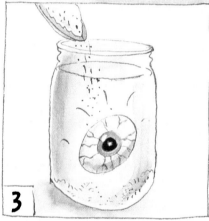

3

Gradually stir one tablespoon of salt after another into the water and watch that eyeball begin to lift off the bottom. Ugh!

DEAD SEA

Fact File ▷▶ Just as the salt in the sea holds you up when you are swimming, the salty water supports the weight of the egg. The saltier the water the better it will float.

The Incredible Rubber Egg

How do you take off the shell of a hard-boiled egg without cracking it? It's very simple and here's how.

What you will need:
- 1 hard-boiled egg, with shell on
- glass of vinegar

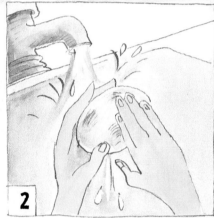

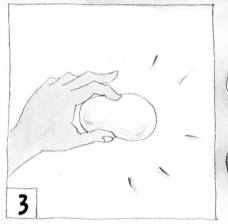

1 Put the egg into the vinegar. Leave it undisturbed for 3 days. You will see some wonderful scum!

2 Take the egg out of the vinegar and rinse it off. The shell will rub off.

3 Give the egg a poke with your finger. Squeeze it gently. What does it feel like? It may even bounce!

Fact File ▷▶ The acidic vinegar "eats up" the calcium carbonate shell, leaving just the inner membrane, or skin, of the egg behind. This makes it feel very rubbery.

Salty Stuff

The Magic Ice Cube

Amaze your friends and family with this cool trick.

What you will need:
- 1 ice cube
- glass of cold water
- 6-in length of sewing thread
- salt
- teaspoon

1 Gently put the ice cube into the glass of water. Carefully place one end of the thread across the top of the floating cube.

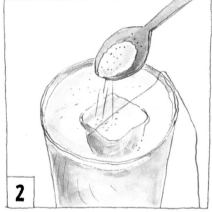

2 Where the thread touches the ice, sprinkle salt over it with a spoon.

3 Wait for about 30 seconds and carefully lift the string. The cube will come too.

Weird or What?
If you piled up all the salt in the world's oceans and seas, it would cover all of Europe with a salt mountain 3 miles deep.

Fact File ▷▶ Because salt lowers the freezing point of water, it melts the ice a little. The thread sinks into a little pool of water which refreezes, trapping the thread.

Crystal Crust

Salt is made of tiny grains, or crystals. You can make your own colony of salt crystals. Don't forget to ask a grown-up to help with the boiling water.

What you will need:
- 1 thick plastic cup
- boiling water
- salt
- tablespoon
- paper towel

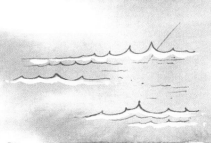

Weird or What?

Believe it or not, 1 quart of blood has the same amount of salt in it as 1 quart of sea water!

Take care! Hot!

1

Ask a grown-up to help you fill the cup with boiling water. Stir in 2–3 tablespoons of salt. Keep adding salt until it stops dissolving.

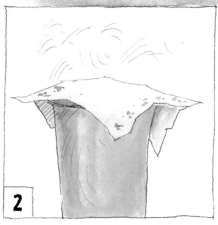

2

Cover the cup with the paper towel and let the water cool. Wait for about 30 minutes.

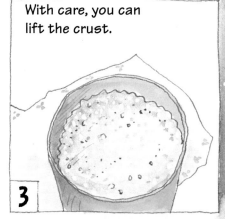

With care, you can lift the crust.

3

Lift the paper and you will see a lovely, solid crust of salt crystals on top of the water.

You can use the magnifier on page 7 to look at the salt crystals more closely.

Fact File ▷▷
Salt crystals will dissolve more easily in warm water than in cold. As the water cools down, some of the salt that dissolved when the water was warm turns back into crystals again.

Whizz, Bang, Burp

Ghastly Gassy Creatures

Watch these monsters expand before your eyes! You can make a whole family of them if you like. Make your designs as big as possible on the unblown-up balloons. To make your own stickers, color in and cut out plain sticky labels.

What you will need:
- balloons
- bought or homemade gruesome stickers (e.g., eyeballs, fangs)
- small funnel
- teaspoon
- baking soda
- vinegar
- small, empty, clean bottles

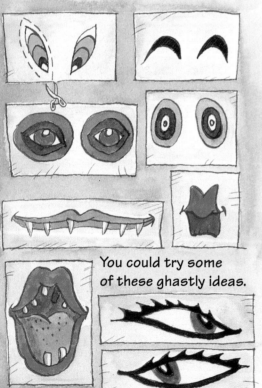

You could try some of these ghastly ideas.

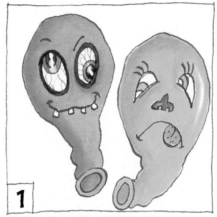

1 Position your stickers firmly on each balloon. Make horrible faces or creatures.

Tap the funnel to help it go down.

2 Using the funnel, spoon 3 heaping teaspoons of baking soda into each balloon.

3 Fill each bottle, a third full, with vinegar and fit the neck of a balloon over each one. Don't let any baking soda fall in yet.

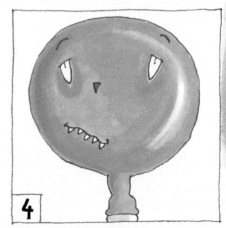

4 Now hold each balloon up and let all the baking soda fall into the vinegar.

Vinegar stings your eyes, so be careful. Wash any spills with plenty of water.

Fact File ▷▶ When the baking soda falls into the vinegar, it causes a chemical reaction that produces carbon dioxide gas. This then blows up the balloon for you.

Balloon Belcher

A simple and safe chemical reaction means you can create some very satisfying sound effects. The vinegary smell makes it even more realistic!

What you will need:
- 1 gassy creature from previous page

1 Carefully ease the balloon, full of gas, off the bottle. Tightly hold the end closed.

2 Slowly let some gas out to make the balloon burp. Practice will make perfect!

Weird or What?
Bacteria in your intestines can produce as much as 1 quart of gas each day!

Slimy World

Create a slithery worm paradise. To find your slimy friends look in freshly dug soil, under large stones and logs, or anywhere damp and shady. See if you can spot worm tunnels—swirls of earth made as soil passes through a worm's body—deposited on the surface.

What you will need:

- shoebox with lid
- masking tape
- pencil
- large empty plastic bottle
- scissors
- 3–4 large beakers of soil
- 1–2 large beakers of sand
- leaves and grass
- 3–4 fat earthworms

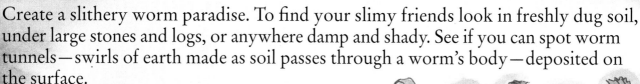

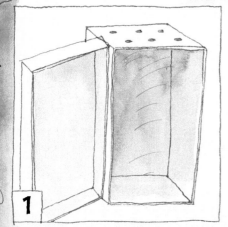

1 Tape the lid to the box to make a "door". Push the pencil into the top of the box to make air holes.

Ask an adult to help with cutting.

Don't make it too damp.

2 Cut the top off the bottle and fill it with alternating layers of soil and sand. Sprinkle with water.

Handle your worms gently.

3 Place some leaves and grass on top. Gently place your worms on them.

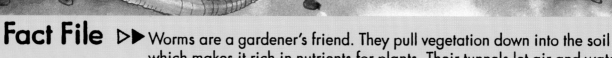

Fact File ▷▶ Worms are a gardener's friend. They pull vegetation down into the soil which makes it rich in nutrients for plants. Their tunnels let air and water into the earth, too.

Weird Worm Fact

Giant earthworms up to 10 feet long can be found in Australia, South Africa and South America. Just think how much soil a worm that size can shift!

4 Put the bottle in the box and close the "door". Leave in a shed or cool, dark place for 4–5 days.

5 Open the "door" and you will see your worms have made tunnels through the soil and sand layers and pulled some food down with them.

Worm Health Warning

Please set your worms free after a few days!

Volcanic Eruption

Make your own volcanic special effects using the simplest of ingredients. It's best to wear old clothes while doing this experiment, and to do it outside.

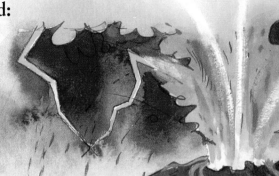

What you will need:
- old newspapers
- damp sand
- baking soda
- small bottle
- funnel
- vinegar
- ketchup
- tablespoon
- small pitcher

Weird or What?

The greatest volcanic eruption ever recorded was on the island of Krakatoa in Indonesia in 1883. The sound of it was heard over 3,000 miles away in Australia, and it made a gigantic tidal wave that killed more than 36,000 people. The wave was even noticed as far away as the English Channel!

The sand should come up to the top of the bottle.

1

Fill the bottle halfway with the baking soda. Then place it on the newspapers and pile up the sand around it to form a small volcano.

2

Put about half the small bottle's worth of vinegar into the pitcher and mix in about 2 tablespoons of ketchup.

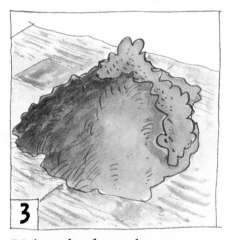

3

Using the funnel, pour the ketchup mixture into the buried bottle—and stand back!

Fact File ▷▷ The acidic vinegar reacts with the alkaline bicarbonate of soda to make a gas—carbon dioxide—which pushes the mixture up out of the bottle.

Underwater Fountain

Create a colorful underwater show. Use any food coloring you like. If you don't have a large bowl or tank you can use a pitcher and one bottle to make a solo show.

What you will need:
- large glass pitcher, a tank, or large clear plastic bowl
- 2–3 small glass bottles
- 2–3 different types of food coloring

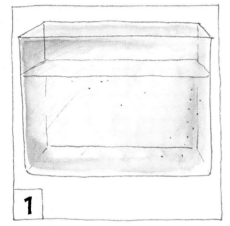

1 Pour cold water into the pitcher, bowl, or tank until it is three-quarters full.

2 Fill the bottles with warm water and add different colored food coloring to each.

3 Place the bottles in the tank so that the tops are well below the surface. Now watch the swirling show.

Upside-down Fountains

Drop ice cubes made from colored water into a pitcher of cold water. At first they will float, but as the ice melts colored water will swirl downward, because it is colder than the water around it.

Fact File ▷▶ Warm water rises and cold water sinks. This is why the warm, colored water rises, and why the cold colored water drifts to the bottom.

Invisible Ink

Write up your scientific notes so that no one else can see them. You can use onion juice instead of lemon but you may cry a lot!

What you will need:
- 1 lemon
- small bowl
- plain white paper
- fine paintbrush or old, empty fountain pen
- oven mitts or pair of kitchen tongs

1
Squeeze the lemon juice into the bowl. Dip in your brush or pen and write on the paper.

2 3-5 minutes
Ask a grown-up to help put the paper into an oven pre-heated to 325°F. Let bake for 3-5 minutes.

3
Ask a grown-up to remove the paper from the oven. Have the oven mitts ready because the paper will be hot! Let it cool off!

Fact File ▷▶ The heat of the oven "burns" the lemon juice. This makes it reappear like magic.

Ectoplasmic Gunk

One minute this gunge behaves like liquid, then it's a solid—wacky stuff! Make as much of this as you like and use any food coloring you want.

What you will need:
- cornmeal
- bowl
- pitcher of water with food coloring added
- tablespoon

1 Put some cornmeal in the bowl and add a little colored water. Stir well.

2 Gradually add more water until the gunk is about as thick as mayonnaise.

3 Jab in your spoon, or squish it in your hands, and it will feel solid. Stir it gently, or scoop some up in your hand, and it's liquid!

Fact File ▷▶ The ectoplasm behaves like a liquid when you treat it gently as all the particles of cornmeal can slide around each other. Squeezing it in your hands makes all the cornmeal particles come together and act like a solid.

Jumping Bugs

Static electricity turns these little insects into jitter bugs. You could try using bug or insect stickers on the paper instead of drawing your own.

What you will need:
- colored tissue paper
- markers or bug stickers
- scissors
- balloon

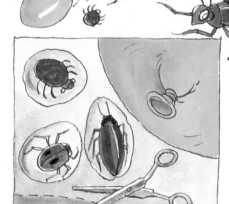

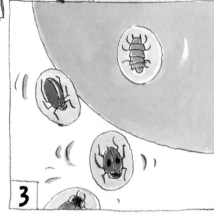

1 Draw some tiny, scary bugs or stick your bug stickers on the tissue paper. Make a lot of them.

2 Cut them out and pile them up. Blow up the balloon and tie the end in a knot.

3 Rub the balloon on top of your head or on your clothes. Hold it above the bugs and watch 'em jump.

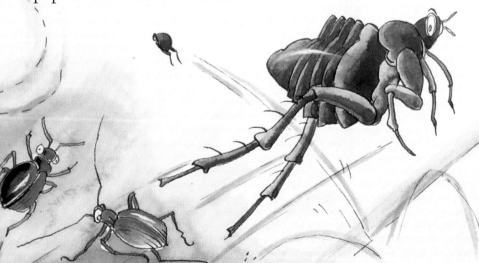

Weird or What?
The average flea can jump 200 times its own height! Just imagine how high we could jump if we were fleas!

Fact File ▷▷ Static electricity is made when some materials are rubbed together—like a balloon against your hair or a wool sweater. It is this kind of electricity that makes the paper jump toward the balloon.

Professor Brainstorm Cocktail

Impress your friends with this fantastic fizzer!
You probably have to be a mad scientist to drink it—
but it is quite safe to try a little.

What you will need:

- glass of cold water, three-quarters full
- few drops of food coloring (your choice of color!)
- 1½ heaping tablespoons powdered sugar
- 3 heaping teaspoons baking soda
- 6 teaspoons lemon juice

1

Add the food coloring to the water.

Do this where spilling doesn't matter.

2

Stir in the sugar and baking soda.

3

Finally add the lemon juice and watch it fizz.

Fact File ▷▷ The acidic lemon juice and alkaline baking soda react to make a gas—carbon dioxide or CO_2. This is the gas that puts the fizz into carbonated drinks.

The Amazing Twister

This is very simple and very curly!

What you will need:
- Scotch tape
- scissors
- heavy-duty aluminum foil
- small desk lamp

Do not touch the lightbulb with fingers or foil.

1 Carefully position a piece of Scotch tape along the edge of the foil. Trim it.

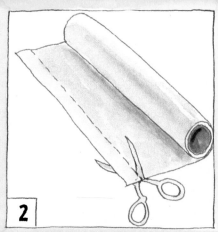

2 Cut off the strip of Scotch tape with aluminum foil stuck to one side.

3 Tape one end to a desktop or table and hold the lamp close to it. Just watch it start to curl and twist as the foil heats up.

Fact File ▷▶ When metal is heated it expands, but plastic does not. When metal foil and Scotch tape are stuck together, the expanding foil forces the tape to curl.

Fake Fossil Footprint

Create a fascinating piece of fossil evidence. Make a cast of a footprint or weird shape to convince your friends that something strange and prehistoric once haunted the neighborhood. If you like, you can use mud instead of a box of sand.

What you will need:
- 1 cup of cold water
- 2 cups of plaster of Paris (from a hardware store)
- bowl or old plastic pot
- small cardboard box with about 3 inches of sand in it

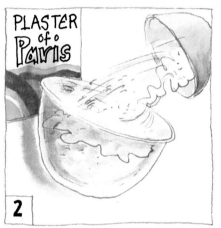

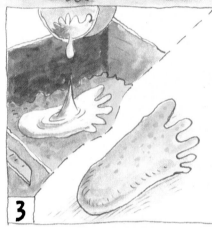

1 Press the shape of your print into the sand or mud using your hands, feet or any other interesting-shaped object.

2 Pour the water into the bowl and sprinkle the plaster over it. Leave for 2 minutes. Then mix well. With clean hands, smooth any lumps. Let stand for 4 minutes.

3 Pour the plaster into your shape, and clean the bowl right away. Let the plaster set, then lift out your fossil evidence.

Fact File ▷▶
Fossils are the preserved remains or traces of plants and animals. Without them we would not know what prehistoric creatures looked like or when they lived. A trace fossil—like a dinosaur footprint—is the mark made by an animal while it was alive, preserved in later soil and rock.

Pus-filled Boil

A gross experiment to test the nerve of your best friend.

What you will need:
- red and yellow (or green) food colorings
- some cotton swabs
- Vaseline
- teaspoon
- small bowl
- a tissue

1 Choose where you want your oozing boil to be, and paint a little red food coloring onto the skin.

Use a fresh cotton swab for mixing.

2 Mix some Vaseline with the yellow or green coloring in the bowl. Put a blob onto the red food coloring patch.

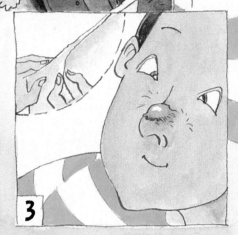

3 Tear a single layer of tissue to fit over the blob. Place on top and seal the "pus" inside, smoothing down the edges of "skin".

Dead SKIN

Weird or What?
Your skin never stops growing. Dead skin falls off, takes the dirt with it, and more skin cells are constantly produced. About 9 pounds of skin flakes off you every year. Dust is mostly made up of old bits of you!

Fact File ▷▷
Pus is putrid stuff. It is made of infection-fighting body fluids, dead cells, and dead bacteria.